HOLIDAY SONG BOOK

Piano Accompaniments by
John Van Buskirk
Smith College

© 1988 by Holt, Rinehart and Winston, Publishers
Printed in the United States of America

0-03-005253-X

890 018 987 65432

Acknowledgments for previously copyrighted material appear with
the material used.

Table of Contents

We Shall Not Be Moved

Labor Day

Traditional

The un-ion is be-hind us, we shall not be moved, The un-ion is be-hind us, we shall not be moved, Just like a tree that's plant-ed by the riv - er, We shall not be moved.

We shall not be, we shall not be moved, We shall not be, we shall not be moved, Just like a tree that's plant-ed by the riv - er, We shall not be moved.

American Indian Day

Navajo Happy Song

Recorded by M. Twohy

Navajo Song

Hi yo hi yo ip si ni yah, hi yo

hi yo ip si ni____ yah, hi____ yo hi yo ip si ni yah,

hi____ yo hi yo ip si ni yah. Ip si ni YAH!

Seeyahnah

American Indian Song*

Seeyahnah, seeyahnah, seeyahnah, seeyahnah, Seeyahnah ya ho, Seeyahnah ya ho.

*May be sung as a round.

The Gift of Peace

Otoe Song

Zhin-ga-dha-we dho____ dho we he____ ho - i - ne

Zhin-ga-dha-we dho____ dho we____ he____ ho-i - ne

Zhin-ga-dha-we dho____ dho we ha je dha we.

6

Rosh Hashanah

L'Shono Tovo

Traditional

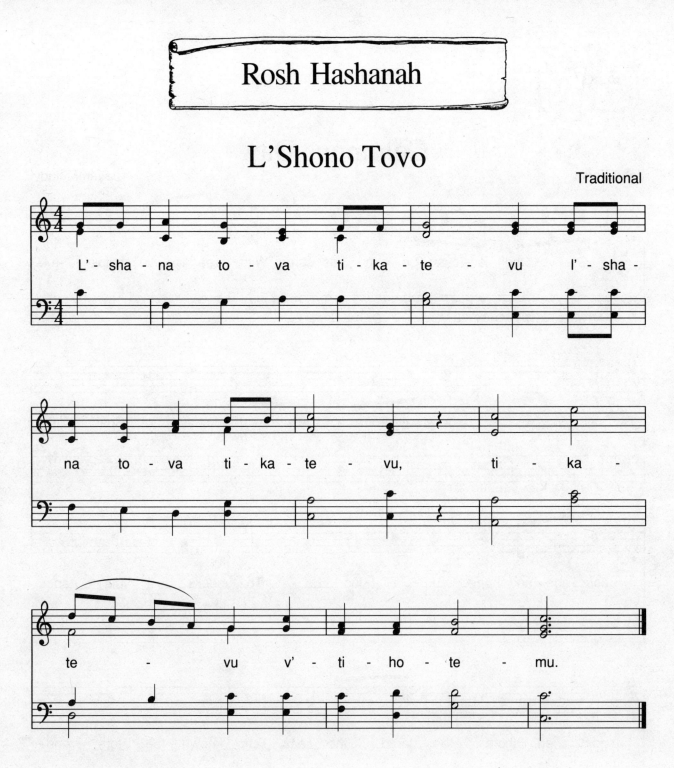

L'- sha - na to - va ti - ka - te - vu l'- sha -
na to - va ti - ka - te - vu, ti - ka -
te - vu v'- ti - ho - te - mu.

Translation: Happy New Year to you and yours.

Columbus Day

Columbus Day

John Erwin   Italian Melody

O - ver the o - cean Co - lum - bus came, With three lit - tle ships a -

sail - ing;____ A - way from a town on the coast of Spain, With

cour - age and hope un - fail - ing.____ To seek__ a dis - tant

gold - en shore He dared__ the seas un - known be - fore; And

ev - er he pi - lot - ed west - ward Three lit - tle ships a - sail - ing.____

United Nations Day

Carol of Service

Steuart Wilson

French Folk Song

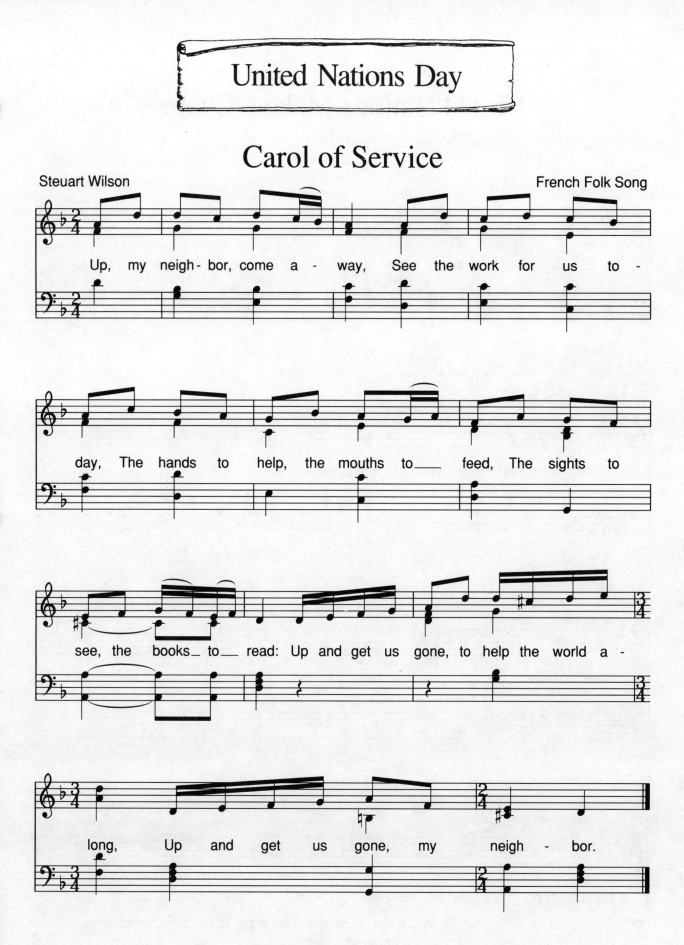

Up, my neigh- bor, come a - way, See the work for us to -
day, The hands to help, the mouths to_ feed, The sights to
see, the books_ to_ read: Up and get us gone, to help the world a -
long, Up and get us gone, my neigh- bor.

United Nations Make a Chain

Tom Glazer

Tune: Hold On

Halloween

(It's a) Monster's Holiday

Words and Music by
Buck Owens

Frank - en - stein was the first in line___ and the wolf - man came up next.___ Dra - cu - la was a - do - in' his stuff a - breath - in' down___ my neck! Jump back,___ make tracks, here comes the hunch - back, bet - ter get out of his way, Fe - fe - fi - fi - fo - fo - fum, it was a

good - ness what an aw - ful sight.___ I said, "Good

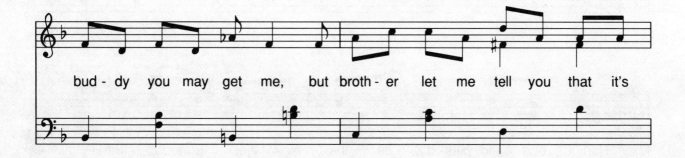

bud - dy you may get me, but broth - er let me tell you that it's

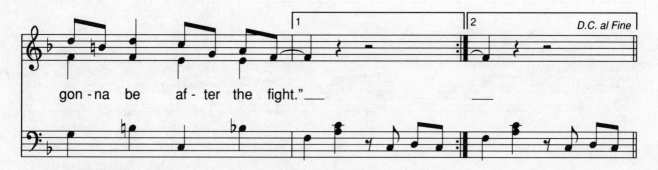

gon - na be af - ter the fight."___

2. Uncle Bill, well he took ill. and they sent for me to come.
   Well, I had to pass by the old graveyard so I went on the run.
   There was screamin' and moanin', wailin' and groanin', scary as a mummy's curse.
   I said, "Good buddy you may get me, but brother let me tell you that you're gonna have to catch me first."

Hail to the Chief

Sir Walter Scott and
James Sanderson

Maestoso

Hail to the Chief who in tri - umph ad - vanc - es!

Hon - or'd and bless'd be the ev - er - green___ Pine!

Long may the tree, in his ban - ner that glanc - es,

Flour - ish, the shel - ter and grace of our line!

Although the words are of Scottish origin, this melody is played to honor the President of the United States.

Thanksgiving

Let Us Break Bread Together

Black Spiritual

1. Let us break bread to-geth-er on our knees,

Let us break bread to-geth-er on our knees.

When I fall on my knees with my face to the ris-ing

sun, O Lord, have mer-cy on me.

2. Let us praise God together on our knees. *(etc.)*

• "Let Us Break Bread Together," arranged by Augustus D. Zanzig, from JR HIGH SING, World Around Songs. Reprinted by permission.

For the Beauty of the Earth

Folliot S. Pierpont

Arr. from Conrad Kocher

1. For the_ beau - ty of the earth, For the beau - ty of the skies,
2. For the_ beau - ty of each hour Of the day and of the night,
3. For the_ joy of hu - man love, Broth - er, sis - ter, par - ent, child,

For the_ love which from our birth O - ver and a - round us lies,
Hill and_ vale, and tree and flow'r, Sun and moon, and stars of light,
Friends on_ earth and friends a - bove, For all gen - tle thoughts and mild,

Lord of all, to Thee we raise This our hymn of grate - ful praise.

Chanukah

Hayo, Haya

Chanukah Song

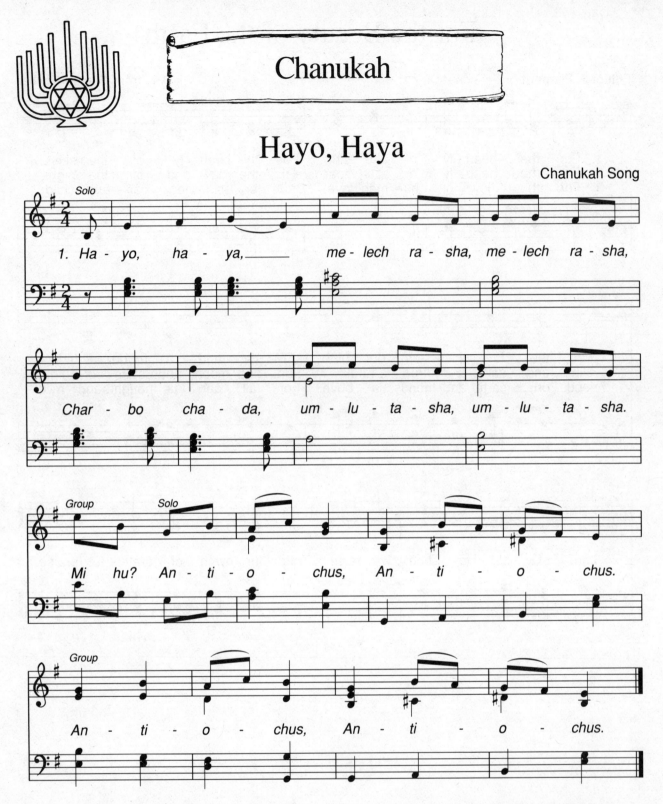

1. Ha - yo, ha - ya,___ me - lech ra - sha, me - lech ra - sha,
Char - bo cha - da, um - lu - ta - sha, um - lu - ta - sha.
Mi hu? An - ti - o - chus, An - ti - o - chus.
An - ti - o - chus, An - ti - o - chus.

1. Hayo, haya, melech rasha, melech rasha,
   Charbo chada, umlutasha, umlutasha.
   Group: Mi hu? Solo: Antiochus, Antiochus.
   Group: Antiochus, Antiochus.

2. Kam ish gibor, shmo Yehuda, shmo Yehuda,
   Hitsil artso hachamuda, hachamuda.
   Group: Mi hu? Solo: Hamakkabi, Hamakkabi.
   Group: Hamakkabi, Hamakkabi.

3. Ba l'mikdash, hidlik m'nora, hidlik m'nora,
   V'lay'hudim hayta ora, hayta ora.
   Group: Matay? Solo: baChanukka, baChanukka.
   Group: baChanukka, baChanukka!

1. Once there was a wicked, wicked king,
   His sword was sharp, his darts did sting.
   What was his name?—Anti-ochus!

2. Rose the hero, Judah the brave,
   His ancient land to save, to save.
   What was his name?—the Maccabee!

3. In the Temple he lit the Menorah, Menorah,
   And then the Jews had light, had Torah.
   When was this?—On Chanukah!

Mi Y'malel?

Chanukkah Song

Mi y'-mal-el g'vu-rot Yis-ra-el? O-tan mi yim-ne?

Hen b'chol dor ya-kum ha-gi-bor Go-el ha-am.

Shma!_____ Ba-ya-mim ha-hem ba-z'man ha-

ze,_____ Mak-ka-bi mo-shi-a u-fo-

de._____ Uv'-ya-mey-nu, kol am Yis-ra-

el,_____ Yit-a-ched ya-kum l' hi-ga-

el!_____

D.C. al Fine

Translation:

Who can retell your feats, Israel?
Who can count them all?
Throughout the years, a hero appears,
To save us. Recall:

At this very time so long ago,
Maccabee arose and smote the foe.
The whole people in our time as well,
Will unite and build free Israel.

Christmas Eve

Cordelia B. Fenno

English Folk Song

On the ground the snow-flakes glis-ten,

This is the eve of Christ-mas; Bells are

chim-ing as we lis-ten, This is the eve of

Christ-mas; The i-ci-cles hang a-bove our

heads, And this is the eve of Christ-mas.

From Heaven Above

Translated by C. Carlin

German Carol

1. From heav - en a - bove the an - gels come. Ah, _____

ah, _____ Ho - san - nah, ho - san - nah, sing all we, Come

sing and strum, and play _ your drum, Al - le - lu - ja, al -

le - lu - ja, Sing of the Christ Child and Ma - ry.

2. The voice of the lute should sound soft and sweet, Ah, etc.
   So that the Child may fall asleep, Alleluja, etc.

3. On earth be peace, fraternity, Ah, etc.
   Praise God in all eternity, Alleluja, etc.

• "From Sky Above," translation by Charlotte Carlin, from THE DITTY BAG, by Janet E. Tobitt. Reprinted by permission of Girl Scouts of the U.S.A.

In Dulci Jubilo

German Melody

We've Been a While A-Wandering

Yorkshire Christmas Carol

We've been a while a-wan-der-ing a-
We are not dai-ly beg-gars that

mongst the leaves so green,_____ But now we come a-
beg from door to door;_____ We are your neigh-bor's

was - sail-ing, so plain-ly to be seen,
chil - dren, for we've been here be - fore. For it's

Christ-mas time, when we trav-el far and near. May God

bless you and send you A hap-py New____ Year.____

To Bethlehem, Singing

A Belén Cantando

Puerto Rican Carol

1. The Vir-gin was at ease and hap-py in the sta-ble,___
1. *La Vir-gen mi-ra - ba con gus-to y ca-ri - ño*___

___ The ox-en si-lent vi - gil keep-ing o'er the cra-dle.
___ *Que el bu-ey vi-gi-la - ba la cu-na del ni - ño.*

REFRAIN

To Beth-le-hem, sing - ing down from Heav'n did fall_____
A Be-lén can-tan - do del cie-lo ba-jó

___ To tell the_ ti-dings joy-ous-ly to all,___ joy-ous-ly to all.
___ *Va-mos a-nun-cian - do que el ni-ño na-ci ó,___ que el ni-ño na-ci ó.*

2. To shepherds came a voice while they their flocks were tending,
"This night the holy Son of Mary I am sending."

2. *Del cielo bajó una voz que decía*
Ahi le mando yo al hijo de María.

On This Day

Words by M.L. May

Ancient Plainsong

On this day, let songs ring! Sweet and clear, chil-dren sing.
Per - son - ent ho - di - e Vo - ces pu - er - u - lae,

Praise the babe, Christ, the king, Born of maid - en low - ly,
Lau - dan - tes ju - cun - de Qui no - bis est na - tus,

Son of God, most ho - ly. Id - e - o - o - o, id - e - o -
Sum - mo De - o da - tus.

o - o, Id - e - o glo - ri - a in ex - cel - sis De - o!

New Year's Day

Auld Lang Syne

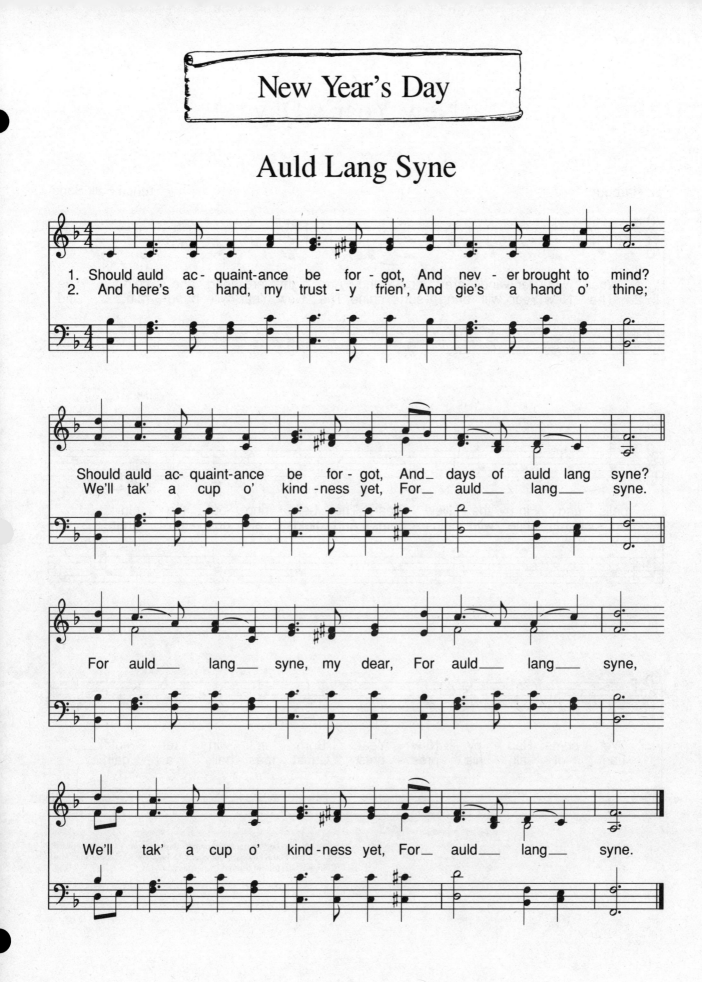

1. Should auld ac-quaint-ance be for-got, And nev-er brought to mind?
2. And here's a hand, my trust-y frien', And gie's a hand o' thine;

Should auld ac-quaint-ance be for-got, And days of auld lang syne?
We'll tak' a cup o' kind-ness yet, For auld lang syne.

For auld lang syne, my dear, For auld lang syne,

We'll tak' a cup o' kind-ness yet, For auld lang syne.

New Year's Day

H. Harbour

French Folk Song

1. When win-ter winds are blow-ing, And nights are long and cold,___ The
2. The New Year will bring sun-shine, The New Year will bring rain;___ And

bells ring in the New Year, The bells ring out the old.___
or-chards white with blos-soms, And fields of gold-en grain.___

Wel-come, Hap-py New Year, Born in win-ter cold!___
Last of all his pres-ents, Christ-mas bells a-gain.___

• "New Year's Day," words by Homer H. Harbour from CONCORD SERIES NO. 7, 140 FOLK SONGS, copyright © 1922 by E. C. Schirmer Music Company, Boston. Reprinted by permission.

The Old Year Now Away Is Fled

Traditional tune.
Words adapted by Percy Dearmer

The old year now__ a-way is fled,__ The new year it__ is en - ter - èd; Then let us now__ our sins down - tread,__ All joy - ful - ly all__ ap - pear: Let's mer - ry be this day,__ And let us now__ both sport and play: Hang grief,__ cast care a - way! God send you a hap - py New Year!__

We Shall Overcome

Traditional

We shall o-ver-come,___ We shall o-ver-come,___
We'll walk hand in hand,___ We'll walk hand in hand,___

We shall o-ver-come some day;_____ Oh!___
We'll walk hand in hand some day;_____

Deep in my heart, I do be-lieve,

We shall o-ver-come some day._____
We'll walk hand in hand some day._____

Abraham, Martin, and John

Words and Music by
Dick Holler

we'll be free. Some day soon it's gon-na be___ one day. Has

an - y - bod - y here seen my old friend Bob - by,___

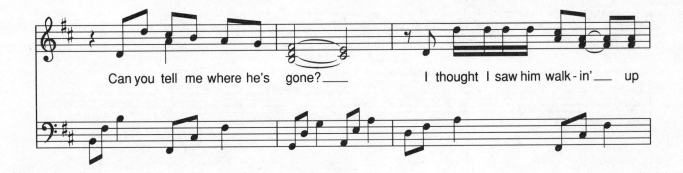

Can you tell me where he's gone?___ I thought I saw him walk - in'___ up

o - ver the hill___ with A - bra - ham, Mar - tin,___ and___ John.

Valentine's Day

St. Valentine's Day

Richard Compton

French Folk Song

1. A - mong the win - ter's hap - py days Comes one in Feb - ru -

a - ry, When old and young send Val - en - tines To

make each oth - er mer - ry; Tra la la la, Tra la la

la, Tra la la la la la la la la la, Tra la la

la, Tra la la la, Tra la la la la la la la la la la.

2. Shop windows full of valentines
   Look just like gardens growing,
   With white and red and pink and blue
   And gold and silver glowing.
   Tra la la la, etc.

Valentines

H. Harbour

Old English Melody

1. In the dark of the win-ter when cold winds do blow, Saint
2. There are hearts and gay rib-bons, and birds on the wing, Gilt,

Val - en - tine's Day comes Like flow'rs in the snow; Bring-ing
lace and red ros - es, With ev - 'ry fine thing; But the

thoughts of our dear ones whose love we re - new, By
love in our hearts send - ing gifts on their way, Is

send - ing them greet - ings of friend - ship still true.
best of all bless - ings on Val - en - tine's Day.

Lincoln's Birthday

Homer Harbour

Dutch Folk Song

In tow'r and spire were ring - ing, This day at dawn, the bells; And now the chil - dren's sing - ing From hall and school - house swells. Of__ one who lov'd His__ peo - ple The glad birth - day to__ greet: Ring, bells from ev - 'ry stee - ple, Wave, flags in ev - 'ry street!

Washington's Birthday

Homer Harbour

French Folk Song

For the birth - day of a sol - dier all the bells are rung this day; For the birth - day of a states - man all the streets with flags are gay; He was lead - er of our Ar - mies in the long, long, years a - go, When they wan - der'd, cold and bare - foot, in the cru - el win - ter __ snow.

Young George Washington

Anonymous (extended by D.S.)

Early American Song

George Wash - ing - ton he was a can - ny young scout, Sing Hal - i - for Jo if I do;_____ The back of the coun - try he knew all a - bout, Sing nick - el, sing nack - el, sing new;_____ Sing bands and reb - els, and reb - els and trou - bles, Sing new, new.___

Women and the Vote

Tune: Auld Lang Syne

1. I have a neigh-bor, one of those Not ver-y hard to find,

Who know it all with-out de-bate, And nev-er change their mind.

I asked him "What of wom-an's rights?" He said in tones se-vere—

"My mind on that is all made up, Keep wom-en in their sphere."

2. I met an earnest, thoughtful man,
   Not many days ago,
   Who pondered deep all human law,
   The honest truth to know;
   I asked him, "What of women's cause?"
   The answer came sincere—
   "Her rights are just the same as mine,
   Let women choose their sphere."

• "Women and the Vote," from the recording SONG OF THE SUF-FRAGETTES, Folkways Records. Folkways/Smithsonian Sole distributors. Birch Tree Group Ltd. Reprinted by permission.

Purim

Hop! Mayne Homntashn!

Traditional

Yach - ne - Dvo - she fort in mark, Zi halt zich in eyn pa - kn,
Fort oyf Pu - rim koy - fn - mel, Ho - mn - ta - shn

ba - kn. Hop! may - ne ho - mn - ta - shn, Hop! may - ne vay - se.

Hop! mit may - ne ho - mn - ta - shn Hot pa - sirt a may - se!

1. Yachne-Dvoshe fort in mark,
   Zi halt zich in eyn pakn,
   Fort oyf Purim koyfn mel,
   Homntashn bakn.

   Chorus:
   Hop! mayne homntashn,
   Hop! mayne vayse.
   Hop! mit mayne homntashn
   Hot pasirt a mayse!

2. S'geyt a regn, s'geyt a shney,
   Es kapet fun di decher.
   Yachne firt shoyn korn-mel,
   In a zak mit lecher.

   (Chorus)

3. Nisht kayn honig, nisht kayn mon,
   Un fargesn heyvn,
   Yachne macht shoyn homntashn,
   Es bakt zich shoyn in oyvn . . .

   (Chorus)

4. Yachne trogt shoyn shalach-mones,
   Tsu der bobe Yente—
   Tsvey-dray homntashn,
   Halb-roy—halb-farbrente!

   (Chorus)

1. Yachne-Dvoshe's in a dither,
   Packing for the market-place,
   She is off to buy the flour
   For to bake the Purim cakes.

   Ho, my homentashn!
   Ho, my white delights!
   Ho, my homentashn
   Didn't come out quite right!

2. It's raining and it's snowing,
   And the roofs are dripping,
   Yachne's bringing cornmeal home
   In a bag that's ripping.

3. She's brought no honey, no poppy-seed,
   And quite forgot the yeast.
   But Yachne's making homentashn,
   They're in the oven, at least.

4. Yachne's carrying her Purim gift
   To her mother-in-law,
   Two or three homentashn,
   Half-burned and half-raw.

The Wearing of the Green

Traditional

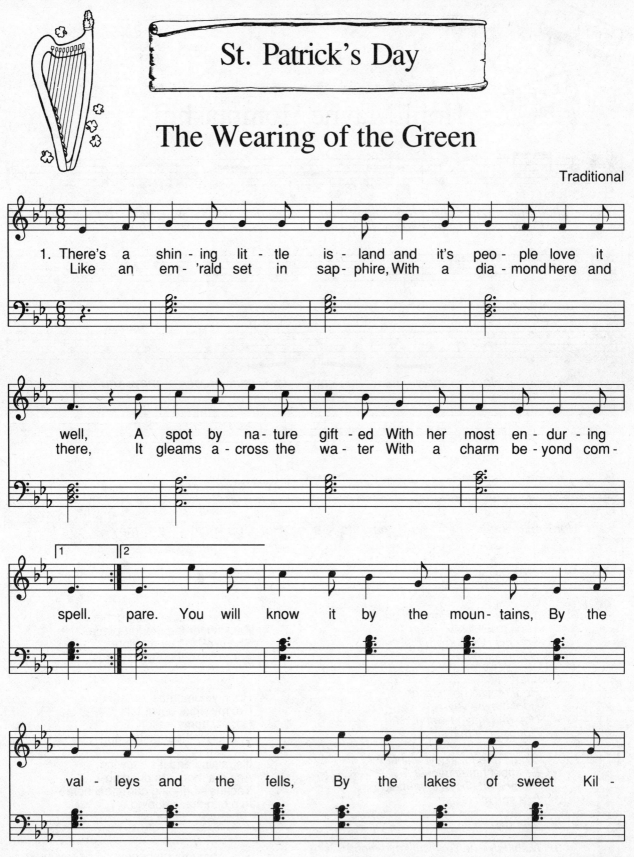

1. There's a shin-ing lit-tle is-land and it's peo-ple love it
Like an em-'rald set in sap-phire, With a dia-mond here and

well, A spot by na-ture gift-ed With her most en-dur-ing
there, It gleams a-cross the wa-ter With a charm be-yond com-

spell. pare. You will know it by the moun-tains, By the

val-leys and the fells, By the lakes of sweet Kil-

lar - ney, Where the blue of heav - en dwells; You will know it by the

sham - rock, Dear - est em - blem ev - er seen, And

know its men and wom - en By the wear - ing of the green.

2. It is famed in song and story,
   'Tis the fount of wild romance,
   The native home of minstrelsy
   Whose measures all entrance;
   Though the bards who made such music
   As the world can ne'er forget,
   Are sleeping long in silence,
   Still their songs are living yet.

The Galway Piper

Irish Folk Song

Ev-'ry per-son in the na-tion,_ Or of great or hum-ble sta-tion,_

Holds in high-est es-ti-ma-tion Pip-ing_ Tim_ of_ Gal-way.

Loud-ly_ he can play or low; He can_ move you fast or slow;

Touch your_ hearts or stir your toe, Pip-ing_ Tim of Gal-way.

2. When he walks the highway pealing,
   Round his head the birds come wheeling,
   Tim has carols worth the stealing,
   Piping Tim of Galway.
   Thrush and linnet, finch and lark,
   To each other twitter, "Hark!"
   Soon they sing from light to dark
   Pipings learnt in Galway.

Arbor Day

The Linden Tree

Wilhelm Müller
Tr. by Theodore Baker

Franz Schubert

By the well be-fore the door-way There stands a lin-den tree, How oft be-neath its shad-ow Sweet dreams have come_ to me; Up-on its bark when mus-ing Fond words of love I made, And joy a-like and sor-row Still drew____ me to its shade.

The Tree in the Wood

Collected by Cecil Sharp

All in__ a__ wood there grew a tree, The fin - est__ tree you

ev - er did see, And the green leaves grew a - round, a - round, a - round,

And the green leaves grew a - round. (2.) And on__ this__ tree there
(3.) on__ this__ limb there
(4.) on__ this__ branch there

was a limb, The fin - est__ limb you ev - er did see, The
was a branch, The fin - est__ branch you ev - er did see, The
was a nest, The fin - est__ nest you ev - er did see, The

limb was on the tree, The tree was in the wood,_____ And the

{ branch was on the limb, The }
  limb was on the tree, The }
{ nest was on the branch, The }
  branch was on the limb, The }
(limb was on the tree, The)

green leaves grew a - round, a - round, a - round, And the

green leaves grew a - round.   3. And
                                4. And

                                        round.

5. And in this nest their was an egg,
   The finest egg you ever did see, etc.,

6. And in this egg their was a yolk,
   The finest yolk you ever did see, etc.,

7. And in this yolk there was a bird,
   The finest bird you ever did see, etc.,

8. And on this bird there was a wing,
   The finest wing you ever did see, etc.,

9. And on this wing there was a feather,
   The finest feather you ever did see,
   The feather was on the wing,
   The wing was on the bird,
   The bird was in the yolk,
   The yolk was in the egg,
   The egg was in the nest,
   The nest was on the branch,
   The branch was on the limb,
   The limb was on the tree,
   The tree was in the wood,
   And the green leaves grew around, around, around,
   And the green leaves grew around.

*This measure is repeated twice in the third verse, three times in the fourth verse, and so on.

Easter Alleluya

W.H. Draper

German Melody

An Easter Hymn

English Words by J. Mattfeld

Vulpius

1. Praise be to God by saints a - dor'd And to His on - ly Son,— our Lord Who for our sins His life out - pour'd. Hal - le - lu - jah!___ Hal - le - lu - jah!___ Hal - le - lu - jah!

2. Help us to live from all sin free,
   That we may bless Thy name and Thee,
   Singing Thy praise eternally,
   Hallelujah! *(Etc.)*

• "An Easter Hymn," English version by J. Mattfeld from CHILDREN'S CAROLS FOR ALL OCCASIONS by Marie E. Walker, Julius Mattefeld, Edwardo Matzo. Reprinted by permission of The Willis Music Company.

On Easter Day

• "On Easter Day," words by John Irwin from CONCORD SERIES NO. 4, A BOOK OF SONGS FOR GRADES IV, V, VI, copyright © 1924 by E. C. Schirmer Music Company, Boston. Reprinted by permission.

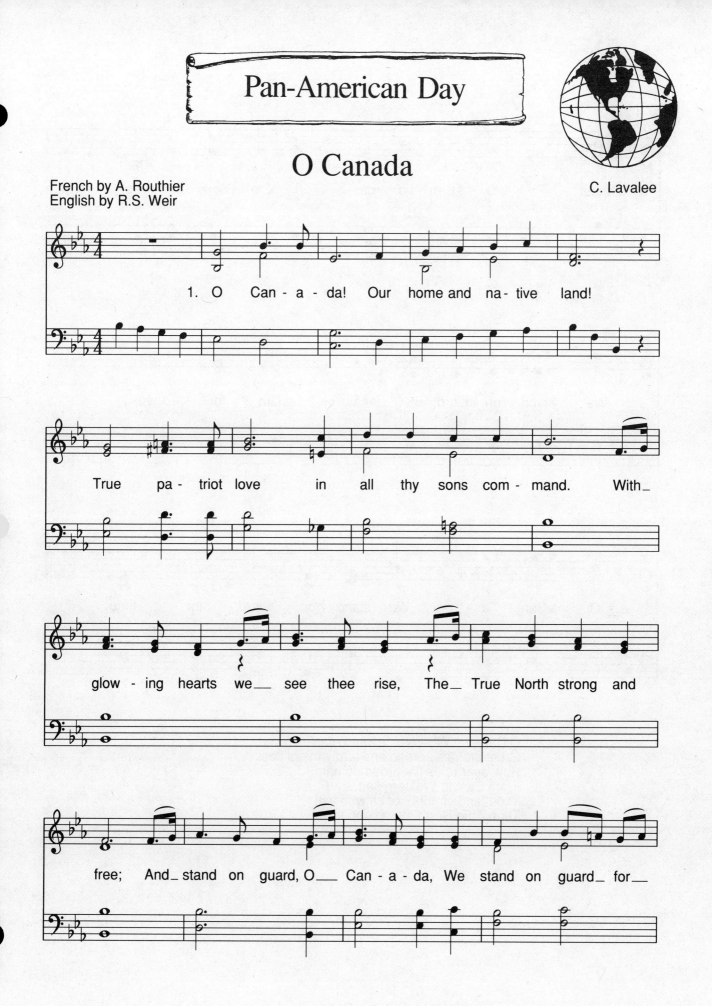

Pan-American Day

O Canada

French by A. Routhier
English by R.S. Weir

C. Lavalee

1. O Can - a - da! Our home and na - tive land!

True pa - triot love in all thy sons com - mand. With

glow - ing hearts we see thee rise, The True North strong and

free; And stand on guard, O Can - a - da, We stand on guard for

2. O Canada! Where pines and maples grow,
Great prairies spread and lordly rivers flow.
How dear to us thy broad domain,
From East to Western sea.
Thou land of hope for all who toil!
Thou True North strong and free.

Morning Song

Las Mañanitas

English Version by
Janet E. Tobitt

Mexican Folk Song

With a morn - ing song we greet you as King
Es - tas son las ma - ña - ni - tas que can -
ehs' - tahs sohn lahs mah - nyah - nee' - tahs kay cahn -

Da - vid used to sing, But more beau - ti - ful than
ta - ba el Rey Da - vid, Pe - ro no e - ran tan bo -
tah' - bah ehl ray dah - veed', peh' - roh noh eh' - rahn tahn boh -

his song____ is the mu - sic we bring.
ni - tas co - mo las can - tan a - quí.
nee' - tahs coh' - moh lahs cahn' - tahn ah - kee'.

Fine

Wake up, then, O my be - lov - ed, wake
Des - pier - ta, mi bien, des - pier - ta, mi -
dehs - pyehr' - tah, mee byehn, dehs - pyehr' - tah, mee

up,   for   the   dawn   is   nigh;   The___   birds   are   sweet - ly
ra   que   ya a - ma - ne - ció,   *Ya   los   pa - ja - ri - llos*
rah'   kay   yah ah- mah - neh - syoh',   yah lohs   pah - hah - ree' - yohs

D.C. al Fine

sing - ing,   the   moon   has   gone   from   the   sky.
can - tan,   la   lu - na   ya   se   me - tió.
cahn' - tahn,   lah   loo' - nah   yah   seh   meh - tyoh'.

May Day

The Cuckoo

Austrian Folk Song

1. Oh I went to the flow - ing spring Where the
2. Af - ter Eas - ter come sun - ny days That will

wa - ter's so good, And I heard there the cuck - oo As she
melt all the snow; Then I'll mar - ry my maid - en fair, We'll be

called from the wood.
hap - py, I know.

Ho - li - ah, Ho - le - rah - hi - hi - ah,

Ho - le - rah cuck - oo! Ho - le - rah - hi - hi - ah,

Ho - le - rah cuck - oo! Ho - le - rah - hi - hi - ah,

Ho - le - rah cuck - oo! Ho - le - rah - hi - hi - ah - ho! *(clap)*

Now Is the Month of Maying

Old English

Thomas Morley

1. Now is the month of May - ing, When mer - ry lads are play - ing,
2. The spring, clad all in glad - ness, Doth laugh at win - ter's sad - ness,

Fa la la la la la la la la, Fa la la la la la la.

1. Each with his bon - ny lass, A - danc - ing on the grass.
2. And to the bag - pipe's sound, The nymphs tread on the ground.

Fa la la la la, Fa la la la la la la la la la la la.

Mother's Day

Love Somebody

American Folk Song

Love my moth-er, yes I do, Love my moth-er, yes I do,
Love my fa-ther, yes I do, Love my fa-ther, yes I do,

Love my moth-er, yes I do, Love my moth-er, oh, I'll tell you.
Love my fa-ther, yes I do, Love my fa-ther, oh, I'll tell you.

REFRAIN

Love my moth-er, yes I do, Love my moth-er, yes I do,
Love my fa-ther, yes I do, Love my fa-ther, yes I do,

Love my moth-er, yes I do, And I know my moth-er loves me too.
Love my fa-ther, yes I do, And I know my fa-ther loves me too.

Memorial Day or Veteran's Day

Memorial Day

R. Compton

Czech Folk Song

1. March-ing proud-ly, March-ing proud-ly, Went our sol-diers out to fight in bat-tle; Now they lie be-neath the flow-ers, Now they lie be-neath the flow-ers.

2. Starry banner,
Starry banner,
Proudly flying over all the city;
'Twas for you men fought so bravely,
'Twas for you men fought so bravely.

• "Memorial Day," words by Richard Compton from CONCORD SERIES NO. 7, 140 FOLK SONGS, copyright © 1922 by E. C. Schirmer Music Company, Boston. Reprinted by permission.

In Memoriam

H. Harbour

Czech Folk Song

Flow'rs from the shad-y green-wood dell,

Flow'rs from the sun-ny hill-side swell

Scat-ter where lie sleep-ing Their last vig-il keep-ing,

Sol-diers who loved their coun-try well.

Flag Day

Wrap the Flag Around Me, Boys

R. Stewart Taylor

Oh__ wrap the flag__ a-round me, boys To die were far more sweet With__ free-dom's star-ry em-blem, boys, To be my wind-ing sheet. In life I lov'd to see it wave And fol-low__ where it led, And now my eyes__ grow dim, my hands would clasp its last bright shred. Then__ wrap the flag__ a-round me, boys, To die were far more

• "Wrap the Flag Around Me, Boys," by R. Stewart Taylor from THE AMER-ICAN TREASURY OF 1004 FOLK SONGS VOL. 1, copyright © 1977 Shat-tinger International Music Corporation. Reprinted by permission.

Father's Day

Haiye Kirumberumbe

Wachago Tribe

sweet __ With free -dom's star - ry em- blem, boys, To be my wind - ing sheet.

Hai- ye ki -rum- be- rum- be. Na ma-ma ma - ri -

da - di. Hai - ye Ki- rum- be- rum- be. Na Ba- ba ma - ri -

da - di. Hai- ye Ki- rum- be rum- be. Ski- kund- ye iim - ba

cresc.

Kiim - bo, Ha Ha Ha Ha Hi - yoo!

sfz

I'm such a happy fellow.   My Daddy is so great — oh.
I have a lovely Mama.   I'm such a happy fellow,
I'm such a happy fellow,   I sing a happy song — oh.

Independence Day

For Patriots' Day

John Erwin

Dutch Folk Song

1. In Con-cord and in Lex-ing-ton The bells rang out one night, "Be-ware the red-coats! On they come, March-ing a-long with a muf-fled drum!" In Con-cord and in Lex-ing-ton The bells rang out one night.

2. In Concord and in Lexington
   Before the sun did rise,
   The Minutemen stood firm and strong,
   Waiting the foe as he rode along,
   In Concord and in Lexington
   Before the sun did rise.

3. In Concord and in Lexington
   Before the sun had set,
   They chased the soldiers of the crown
   Back o'er the road into Boston town,
   In Concord and in Lexington
   Before the sun had set.

• "For Patriots' Day," words by John Erwin from CONCORD SERIES NO. 7, 140 FOLK SONGS, copyright © 1922 by E. C. Schirmer Music Company, Boston. Reprinted by permission.

The Liberty Song

John Dickinson

William Boyce

Come join hand in hand, brave A - mer - i - cans all, And

rouse your bold hearts at fair Li - ber - ty's call; No

ty - ran - nous acts shall sup - press your just claim, Or

stain with dis - hon - our A - mer - i - ca's name.

In Free - dom we're born and in Free - dom we'll live, Our

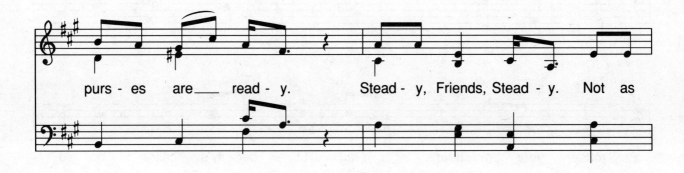

purs - es are___ read - y. Stead - y, Friends, Stead - y. Not as

Slaves,___ but as Free men our mon - ey we'll give.

Alphabetical Index of Songs

TEACHER'S NOTES